# FAILSAFE:
# A CHOREOGRAPHY

**Scott Thurston**'s most recent book is *Turning: Selected Poems 1995-2020* (Shearsman, 2023). Since 2004, he has been developing a practice integrating dance and poetry called *kinepoetics*, which has seen him training and working with professional dancers in the UK and overseas. In 2014 he co-founded the Arts for the Blues project, developing a new creative group psychotherapy for depression. Scott is a person-centred counsellor and Chair in Poetry and Innovative Creative Practice at the University of Salford.

## Also by Scott Thurston

| | |
|---|---|
| *Turning: Selected Poems 1995-2020* | (Shearsman, 2023) |
| *Terraces: a choreography* | (Beir Bua, 2022) |
| *Phrases towards a Kinepoetics* | (Contraband, 2020) |
| *We Must Betray Our Potential* | (The Red Ceilings, 2018) |
| *Draft Vicinity* | (Knives Forks and Spoons, 2017) |
| *Poems for the Dance* | (Aquifer, 2017) |
| *Figure Detached Figure Impermanent* | (Oystercatcher, 2014) |
| *Reverses Heart's Reassembly* | (Veer, 2011) |
| *Songs of Desire and Longing* | (Dusie Collective/Knives Forks and Spoons, 2011) |
| *Internal Rhyme* | (Shearsman, 2010) |
| *Of Being Circular* | (Knives Forks and Spoons, 2010) |
| *Momentum* | (Shearsman, 2008) |
| *Hold: Poems 1994-2004* | (Shearsman, 2006) |
| *Turns* (with Robert Sheppard) | (Ship of Fools/Radiator, 2003) |
| *Fragments* | (The Lilliput Press, 1994) |
| *State(s)walk(s)* | (Writers Forum, 1994) |
| *Poems Nov 89 – Jun 91* | (Writers Forum, 1991) |

# Contents

ISBN: 978-1-916938-52-6

Cover designed by Aaron Kent

Edited and Typeset by Aaron Kent

Cover image: © Giovanni Nitti / Adobe Stock

Broken Sleep Books Ltd
PO BOX 102
Llandysul
SA44 9BG

# Failsafe

Scott Thurston

Broken Sleep Books

*

Amongst them I found behind whenever you remember: prepare a meal for God. A lighter touch, toy soldiers rescale. This edge, again, of how far to dress up, curate and present the desperate and contingent. Realised I'd interpreted space behind as moving backwards.

*

Held at home, air is dance; both truth. How to do it for range, permission, decision? I make it will align not by knowing. At the shed, takes time to distinguish at this stage. Open we fall back. Decision is not levels of safety. No need to dream.

*

Does not get disturbed, doesn't tolerate. Give up some control. Not exactly not knowing. Transition between phrases – content of move. Learn to want more – if the ideal to stay in that space could I take it? Virtual head work, fear has manifested inside the rhythm.

*

Continuation of contempt – various contemporary factions, a less encumbered state. Again today feeling. Daily lines just now, a better foil. The table, the sign, the silent scream. Holes in the space of the words. Awareness and naming of disgust – at least two generations of blocked artists adapt to the idea of the dream.

*

Thinking of reading an idea, a trigger in the body means up. Holding breath, core muscles, works for us. Trying to connect to everyday movement – the invitation to expand passes through us. How to use last night's trigger? Have I rejected it for so long I can't change?

*

How to start to unravel? Cut out from forms into goals: celebrate, complain, commemorate. Slip in a varied formal history to suggest options. Neutral tense hopeful, polarity of body and form. The point of the form of the body is to move. We can't reach partners now.

*

Present inside the moving unfolding: oblivious, aware, hiding. Can't see who's looking. Fall into space as if surrounded by it entirely, move as it. Where is your pleasure? Vulnerable in our headlong progression. Moving with and into: take it in turns to suffer.

*

*for Sarah Oktay*

Softening to receive the space in front: quiet steady flame tending pliant. What have you missed? What do you not see? Comparing a key principle, same game: cross the threshold. Risk shame, transducing spiral of sound, echolocation. Tether yourself, turn the page: taken by eminent domain.

*

*i.m. Louise Woodcock*

In the blue hour: thread inside the available giving being received. Impress, surrender to impulses which do not contradict. In the blue hour, what is it other than to live, drop to integrate? Technique to instigate courage to sink deeply into the real. The blue hour: where does it initiate? Let go of naming.

*

Love and its inevitable plurality: when memory spits in the face of power. Lapwings, sorrel, lady's bedstraw beside the reservoir. It feels like I've done everything right to be here today. Large reverse strides with alternating legs, transferring weight, changing direction. The grass lit by the lantern in the park – as if tenderly enfolding the night – how to be a good friend? How to remember what you love, how to love, how to remember? In our reduced state, mist rising in the field at midnight.

*

Sustained radical simplicity, continuous present, combat burnout. Slow, weighted mind of organs, counter-cultural. What are you touching? Make sense by moving and leaving traces, take responsibility for your physical self.

*

*for Tiago Gambogi*
*'How can we create a decentred self as social reimagining?'*
*— Thomas Kempe*

How to honour our land, be worthy of it? Mud roads, deforested hillsides, hydroelectric dam. Blocking doors. Images of mutilation. The more I expose myself, the more fragile, open; the more I feel safe and protected. The police were friendly and kind.

*

I lose the connection but decide to just leave it. I only land, lean. Your interior is my exterior – what is hidden stays out in full view of the throng. Extraction economy: for me I live there, exceed what it looks like about our ill bodies. Make it rain in the hands, everything depends. Point the way, stand for something – train at night.

Know that life demands: give it across 'gainst all disasters. Earth is my blind in the earth, possibility of sight. Touch accrues to them in the open, envisioned cloudy naming. Just step across – we unfold *as* this: choices familiar and other at once back into space. Bring back home whatever we find in depth: already here, already transformed.

*

*for Jonathan Burrows*

Instead of structure, transition. How to get from one moment to the next and endure what degree of change? One state to another, make each change of place in favour of acts. Transitions become structural, structure ephemeral: the feeling of it. The text reappeared in my body as the faintest version of itself.

*for Andrew Holmes*

Took out but could not get back our relation to above. Allow yourself to be lifted in the morning session of immanence – can we combine the two? But at the same time alive. Buzzard over verge. Heat of presence bound to the quality of no longer ours to be owned. Stalk unattached presence – what do you turn to, to be here?

## IS THE WITNESS DANCING?

yesterday the view
too vulnerable for you
consciously span the bridge

we dive through the centre
the still weekend
occupy that quality

don't get attached, witness
space around and within
where do they coincide?

lie on the floor
not aiming for lightning
but something more

*

All of it given space – hold everything on a line in time, gathered-in. They bring gifts to synthesise and complete: from, in, within; to and from the physical centre. Quiet simple courage moving forward and back towards resolution and unfolding – allow it to be given space.

*

Most last for no reason, the torso in front of my actual torso: expanded, elevated, made up of hot energy, full and implacable. Not everything makes desired content. Fill it with information? Earth makes me cry in chaos. To give an account, transition of loss.

*

Failsafe. Would you seek it if you lost it, realise the secret? Different pitch, rate of change, the birds out of the tree. Things at least related. We do not stop. To not think ahead. Are we together as, or together with? Who knows when you might move your hand down, blind to motion. Body shapes the heart. I am earth moving.

*

Trusting sub-con to enter an object, a room, material of all kinds of orders. By the end of your dance the wave calmed down. The voice of the table – from lying to crawling – let's make it move. He does not respond. Let it elevate me: to be still, an unforgivable vulnerability.

*

Do I have the right body for this? A few folk known by sight: to be witnessed, to go high energy. Accepted as and where I was. Great Salt Lake: a little lustful distraction left over later with a little guilt, a book folded in tissue. Go back to still departs, before you already.

*

With the unbroken circle the globe, leave appearances. Actually making, how detailed, how pure? I was of others, leading from my legs, had rejected earlier, articulated a kind, I accept. I accept lust. I do not accept death. I accept this difficulty with living. I do not accept this fear. I accept this fear.

*

for Bill T Jones

Adapted to living with. Perceived as contained. Might be a garden. These forms lose time, visiting them, noticing how they. Creature of the body, arduous and crazy. Show internal landscape. Don't think something as experience in language. In world setting up obstacle, ambush, sabotage. To have to be in the body in a violent relationship to the world.

Thinking is stopping. Where you become who you. Never stops. Who can think are acting. Every day has to stop, clear. This is what fire looks like. Are they past watching clouds? And who are you to do that? Your responsibility is to create a common.

*for Maggie O'Sullivan*

Secure history enabled. Noting, or rather asking at one point, can I dance you my thoughts? I know this bird because I heard it in your poem. Showing respect to yourself. Remember it always. Extend time to make a different choice. Give the cry into low sun. Pick up a small white feather, true as the world.

Anticipating remembering. Giving me strength. Lapwings in the book the colour of my car. What make it was. Summertime sadness revenge night-time procrastination. Now resuming in the present – here she comes, there is time. A history of shadows.

\*

Difficult hill – who sees only through climbing. When otherwise in me break. Oh knees. Coming down the hill in animal – breaking the tail-light. Not too thick nor too fleet. Are we naming or framing? How to loosen the double-pattern, the pleasure arising? Don't fully grasp it. Could come up with a solid hand rail between the senses and the spirit.

\*

To cry, to stay as long as that writerly dance throws, jumps, turns, hops and stops at the end of the phrase. I remember paradise. Tools of reception, projection, carving the space. Strength of words, phrase upon phrase, accompanying the line leading up to the eye. The eye is lost by us at the end of the phrase.

*

Invocation of aim in that sequence accusatory of form let loose to live. With softness many undertones come back to watching blood moon. To not shy away from how you will be read in a house. Would just not work without that engagement – I took it as you walked off the deck. To let you move inside the hedge, head out of the window.

*

Went towards circling around some sort of understanding emerged across a vast gulf waiting for me. Came by and warned you, sort of believed, trusted, indicated the reaction was for you. Lying in the centre of the stone circle, fear of all the challenges above the about.

Just letting go, connecting with a notional sadness at passing of time, incorporated my phrase. Walked out of the circle towards the south-west stone and out to the edge of the summit. Then turned back. Bright ash berries in the centre, crab apples to the west, to the south.

*

*for Amy Voris*

The feet and the grounding offer articulation; tibia, fibula, malleolus create ankle joint. Talus braces back in the cave, if passing weight, enables leverage down to the ground. Point feet to touch talus, adopt to uneven sentences. Stress is absorbed, to serve the distribution of weight.

In the pre-movement, receiving the mineral body, the dome of the skull. Three types of spine, flight and landing. Pelvis articulates, reaches into space – we are constantly. Grant time to work, take responsibility for your movement – let go in clauses.

*

*for Sabine Kussmaul*

Making a little face running out into space when I was a bit stripped of ego. Fluid letting go fell back breathe in three dimensions. Against the wall pressure feedback. Close to breath. Fell in places. When on the floor, sink a shaft – wrap caps in white, as if the hill has received a piece of cloud. Hands that hold, lose sensitivity when touch pressed into service.

*

*for Jan Thurston*

Resisting the idea of making things to sell – getting an idea and putting it away. I understood leaving it alone for a time, cutting and reversing part of the pattern – having the idea first, then working out what it was for later.

*

Challenging order and relationships: holding back mutual testing. Gill slits in an ancient fish; fluid in cochlea vibrates. Sound found you in space, listening through the spine between movements. Eye, ears, nose, spine meets skull – other creatures would hear it differently. Something else I forgot what it looks like what the body is doing.

*

Field tossed by wind, mind; constructed crudesence. To not go back, no tension between our needs, little glimpses of my material – invisible. Embroidered garden birds – the moment tolerable as it is short, safe, held, met. No need to indulge that tender sadness coming up, as if that's all I ever want. It keeps its flame lit, whether I foundered today or made progress. Returning, generating, deepening a critical path, movement initiation – the privilege to imagine failure.

*

Rich minds mind mine decay, double shadow edged, talk to both fear and courage. Keep the image simple, the tension of different patterns: comparing and fear of overwhelm. Being just felt translated into the heart, just attended to – my body in fear, closing up, protecting itself, going stiff: poor strategies for danger. Initially envisaged challenges of feelings and then a wolf, and then the other side of fear. Accepting the cold energy – compose from here.

*

The structure of the morning copes the mind. Not simulate but evolve, as if not a feeling, receiving, letting it through wide multi-dimensionality. Could it appease, try to integrate into a continuum of meaning? Each phrase examines a different situation. My discovery superimposed in a queue in a dream – relaxing into it, form is just incident. Leave something til tomorrow – finishing touches.

*

Hiding behind a column, memory of our survival, the family group closed into itself. Eluded us in places, behind those trees a bull, a raven, a salmon. What does a body not recall? My neck speaks of plenitude, of initiation, of recapitulation, as if the past and present were familiar. In fact, I'd spoken of the raven, taking the skin off the tongue. Include more of yourself, or less of yourself. The heart holds tones and tensions, and moves to resolve them.

*

Between a clasp and a hold, when leave tarmac to earth, for holding me. On way about feeling about being late, spoiling something perfect, the heart learning. The draw on the system of maintaining these postures, so vary the cadence. Stop and drop and search quiet fire: it's not my anger. Sweater – sand martins could live in it. Perhaps going out of my way to help, but the action about the person.

*

too much of a bad thing
stepped into
the beloved's profundity

beyond attachment
shades between
rejoin the river

keeping the wound open
make up, let go, don't stay
make it right

I'll say and I'll mend it
complicated the laughter
arise from love

*

Forgiveness creates responsibility – mapping anger inside to world outside should level. Trigger finger on the dyke wall. Everybody flying past – articulated flesh and bone – enter the glare. Turn this lever to stop a heart, stepped out and then came back in. Work permit me dialogue, tiny touches, your feelings about what my power represented.

*

Read the landscape slipped away, remote but connected from scratch around a bed. Whether to use an old, neglected toaster. Silent, did not engage: encounters between different parts of self, a serial movement music. The storm stormed into the dream, dreamed.

*

Eye of a crow turning over, passing through. How to inhabit the gravity of seduction? Fall into trust, landing on hands. Looking for the heartmouth, blackbird alarm call, sadness to wash us clean.

*'pure concentrated movement | is the science | of its release'*
*—Gil Ott*

Broke through a pride, we take part in our sadness. The moment of this body is listening. Re-space to loss. So you don't have to be alone walking into the space, as if you could be received by it, held by it. Far away already it all feels. Image gave way to a burst of a bird's arrival; slate-grey clouds in the west brushed by pale pink.

*

Overtaken by fierce and tender sadness, I can't hold on, but I try, and do. Limits of testing the voice against itself, as if being evacuated, displaced. The display of the event, took the floor to celebrate work, reaching back into the past. How paths link, edged with conflict, steep, pitches, plastic boxes. Fleeing from something: shine your light.

*

Ear pressed down a tender knee, the rebound. A path which held them. Institute multidiscipline treatments: someone being put naked into a machine, not sure what was to happen. Do you not think this is a little too much? As if gently giving me back my original reaction, my self making friends with myself, again.

*

*for Emma Liggins*

Memorial cards, living funerals, eating ashes. Cover a lot of ground: name not amongst those who did. The peripatetic anti-slavery between the line, girders of twisted metal on the side of the other reactor. How much they were telling, give way to deep well, discipline of joy. A box now open with a lot of friends inside breaks my heart – can't recall spaciousness, another whirling.

lost part
not deferring joy
the other thing
finished by saying
held by space

*

Trying to draw the pattern by gesture when recording voice. False pitch to lease flat toward the light, covered the whole team in glory. Heart as planet; half corn, half industry. Let the space hold us in a pure loss.

*

Slow reaction to aggression, magnified grasp. Listening to earth listening to myself listening, ground always on the move. People on floor in a circle, going around the edge of a new familiarity – how to continue living in this house? As the Sun largest now, emerges from itself.

*

*for Amy Voris*
reframe into moving reflection
uncertain of its provenance
the first movement forward is
the first movement backward
the challenge of the push

*

But also the yield. Feeling the support of morning prayer in the position where I'm held. Secure attachment: ancient and evolutionary relationship. To ground, to support new configurations of body in space, using the weight to lever into movement. Yielding, leading, reaching to grow the reach, let go of grounding. What are you ready to move on from, let go of?

*

Ambivalence around letting go of what has also served. We'll never know. Started on floor, this really was the start: part measured time and part. Begin end with conclusion, finish with 'what we are waiting for'. Not yet ready to turn. Estimate time elapsing before starting. Was it a kind of prayer? What does it mean to be grounded?

*

*for Dirk Hülstrunk*

May have got pushing in there, I think also reaching, adapted myself to their needs. Park Towers, Dark Powers. Layering in colouring, winds divide over them, saint in the palm. Eastern station, first light. Climbing over railings, at one point calling to you above, out of sight. Delicate activism.

*

*for Nita Little*

Moving | at the speed | of your partner's | attention. Bodymind sore, bodymind save: you imagine *before* you embody. Identify with attentional reach in the dream fight – articulated presence. Move | at the speed | of your | attention. With fascial distribution of peripheral intelligence, re-organise ourselves, shift into new shapes of practice. Be in different bodies, instant instant.

*

*for Simon Whitehead and Noc-turne*

Sitting to receive the essence of the score. Turning away from the Sun. How feet respond to the ground at night. Emerge, form relation. Return to the tree, becoming animal. Word wild grain. Complicated laughter.

*

*for Rita Leduc and Rich Blundell*

Rhythm found you in its continual con-fusion of reciprocity. We erase it like a dance that is gone. Go back and look at the world. Walk under protection. How do we remember to tend, accept love.

*

*for Nita Little*

Dorsal back thinking movement as reading, as listening. Make less of division. Fascial reach into the earth, space filled with a tension. Thin-sliced time, easily moved. Reach into touch from the earth: can I pour my weight into you? Accepting the difference between the speeds of our attention.

*

*'Before you knew you owned it'*
*—Alice Walker*

In a constant dance with earth. Giving my weight fully, it rises to meet me. Branch of a plane bifurcates. Evaluate an icy lake – impertinent, degenerate. Stern moments. After others before, complex at the docks, heading inland. We'll never know ambivalence around letting go of what has also served.

*

knowing the way
us less so
ideal separated from
trans-embodied continuities
looking down
into the well
all around us
looking into
the well
impression
of deepening
more dangerous
than crossing
the field

*

Welcome to my dreams of being allocated to a giant man, the hounds flushing out the foxes in the wood, a two-headed giant brandishing an uprooted tree. Passing my double on the opposite side of the chasm gave way to a giant apple, I even wrote it on my hand. A dance in mask and goggles, a stall laid out with things in abundance. How can I find new roles on release? If there are two modes of social being, how to hold them in balance? The tree, after all, communicates through the breeze.

*

inner winds
leaves rotate
flat in a field
another planet

someone undone
in a dream
had to go down
talking sticks

*

Trying to evaluate costs for setting up: how bodies will be in the work, how to destabilise what's there. Shared ancestors, red thread in heart. Where the work starts, she accepts the choice, hard to ignore. Turn towards, away from, turn back. Enter mountain thin as cloud.

\*

This would change at another time – a zero drop with medial posting. Forgot there was any other information, didn't reread, didn't think there was anything there. The amplification of her line crossed into Indiana, heading west – became moral given wrung out. Feeling structures already different – *some* meaning is possible. You do you. Allow a variety of forms to take place.

\*

Not given but still thought, repeated but distinct, held in an array. A temperate system stranding, oscillating in formed naivety. Mourning a life as if unlived.

\*

in here there is something
no telling to me to be time
suddenly coming to me
to all my relations
waiting by the door

## ACKNOWLEDGEMENTS

Many thanks are due to Andrea Mason for the first appearance of this sequence in *Mercurius Magazine* (2022) and to Jess Chandler for her selection in the anthology *Prototype 4* (2022).

LAY OUT YOUR UNREST

www.ingramcontent.com/pod-product-compliance
Lightning Source LLC
Chambersburg PA
CBHW051742040426
42447CB00008B/1267